FASHION OF THE 1920's COLORING BOOK

By Anna Nadler

© Anna Nadler 2020

ANNA C NADLER

ye olde
UNION
OYSTER
HOUSE
est. 1826
HOUSE
LADIES & GENTS 1826 SEA GRILL
UNION
ANNA C NADLER

L.A. BURDICK CHOCOLATES
L.A. BURDICK
L.A. BURDICK
ANNA NADLER

W N S E
ANNA NADLER ©

RH
ANNA
C
NADLER

ANN C NADLER

RETRO
ANNA NADLER

ANNA
C
NADLER

JAZZ AGE

GREEN DRAGON
TAVERN
1773 - 1776
GREEN DRAGON TAVERN

ANNA
C
NADLER

ANNA
C
NADLER

· TREMONT · TEMPLE ·
ANNA C NADLER

JACOB WIRTH
JACOB WIRTH CO.
31-37
JACOB WIRTH
CO-
Restaurant
ANN C HADLEY

OLD CITY HALL
ANNA C WADLER

TASTE THE
5 Historic Teas
THROWN OVERBOARD
AT THE BOSTON
TEA PARTY

About the Artist

Anna Nadler is an illustrator, graphic designer and author, who lives
and works in New York City. She loves drawing fashion, people,
animals and architecture, as well as creating unique logo designs
for various companies from around the world. You can view more of
her work on her website - annanadler.com and on social media
platforms. You can also find many of her original art books in her
Amazon book store, where she is always adding new coloring books,
art tutorials, children's books, gift books, planners and more.
In her free time Anna loves traveling, singing jazz songs and
spending quality time with her friends and family.

Thank you for coloring this book!
If you enjoyed it, please leave a review
on Amazon!